THE BEST OF IRISH MUSIC
COMPLETE SHEET MUSIC EDITIONS

THE ONLY IRISH BOOK YOU'LL EVER NEED!
81 OF THE BEST IRISH SONGS!

Catalog No. 07-1063
ISBN# 1-56922-002-6

EXCLUSIVELY DISTRIBUTED BY

Visit Hal Leonard Online at
www.halleonard.com

CONTENTS

DANNY BOY

Words by Fred Weatherly
Music from An Old Irish Air

Andante

Oh, Dan - ny Boy, the pipes, the pipes are call - ing.... From glen to glen, and down the moun - tain side,........ The sum - mer's

4

PEG O' MY HEART

Words by Alfred Bryan
Music by Fred Fischer

BELIEVE ME IF ALL THOSE ENDEARING YOUNG CHARMS

Traditional

BY KILLARNEY'S LAKES AND FELLS (Killarney)

By E. Falconer and Michael William Balfe

VOICE

1. By Kil-lar-ney's — lakes and fells, Em-'rald isles and —
2. In-nis-fal-len's — ru-in'd shrine May sug-gest a —
3. No place else can — charm the eye With such bright and —
4. Mu-sic there for — Ech-o dwells, Makes each sound a —

1. wind-ing bays, Moun-tain paths, and — wood-land dells,
2. pass-ing sigh, But man's faith can — ne'er de-cline
3. va-ried tints; Ev-'ry rock that — you pass by,
4. har-mo-ny; Man-y voic'd the — cho-rus swells,

COME BACK TO ERIN

By Claribel

15

THE DEAR LITTLE SHAMROCK

Words by Andrew Cherry
Music by J. W. Cherry

2. That dear little plant still grows in our land,
   Fresh and fair as the daughters of Erin,
   Whose smiles can bewitch, and whose eyes can command,
   In each climate they ever appear in:
   For they shine thro' the bog, thro' the brake, and the mireland,
   Just like their own dear little Shamrock of Ireland.
   The dear little Shamrock, the sweet little Shamrock,
   The dear little, sweet little Shamrock of Ireland.

3. That dear little plant that springs from our soil,
   When its three little leaves are extended
   Denotes from the stalk we together should toil,
   And ourselves by ourselves be befriended.
   And still thro' the bog, thro' the brake, and the mireland,
   From one root should branch, like the Shamrock of Ireland.
   The dear little Shamrock, the sweet little Shamrock,
   The dear little, sweet little Shamrock of Ireland.

DUFFY'S BLUNDERS

Words and Music by Joseph Flynn

knew he was guil-ty of course, These words from the Judge made him dance.
good and the bur-glar sent back, With the mules he had stol en a-way.
up on the bench like a Lord, In a few words he set-tled the strife.

CHORUS

1. Young man, I dis-charge you, go run a-way home, I'll let you off this time, you're
2. So he pray'd in the night, and he pray'd ev'-ry day, And soon the good Lord sent the
3. "I move we dis-charge him, we need him in town," Then he spoke out the words which have

free now to roam. For the ev-i-dence shows me right here at a glance, That we
bur-glar his way. But he came in the night-time for he was no fool, And
gained him re-nown. We have two Chi-nese laun-dry-men ev-'ry-one knows, So we'll

can't make a suit out of one pair of pants. 2. Judge
while Duf-fy slept, stole his oth-er blind mule. 3. Now
save the poor black-smith and hang one of those.

4th Verse: When Duffy was poor, sure one day he got work,
For to put in sixteen ton of coal,
He was promised five dollars when he would get through,
So he soon had the coal down the hole.
When he got through the job he went up with a smile,
For his five dollar note he did call,
He was offered one dollar and told with a laugh,
He could take that, or nothing at all.

4th Chorus: But Duffy said "no" and went down in the rain,
And he carried each lump of coal up again,
The poor man was half dead, when he gazed at the heap,
But he says "I'm no gawk and I'll never work cheap."

THE FOGGY DEW

Words by Alfred Percival Graves
Music From An Old Irish Air

THE GALWAY PIPER

An Old Irish Melody

1. Ev - 'ry per - son in the na - tion or of great or hum - ble sta - tion holds in high - est es - ti - ma - tion Pip - ing Tim of

2. When the wedding bells are ringing
   His the breath to lead the singing,
   Then in jigs the folks go swinging.
   What a splendid piper!
   He will blow from eve to morn,
   Counting sleep a thing of scorn.
   Old is he but not outworn
   Knowing you such a piper?

3. When he walks the highway pealing
   'Round his head the birds come wheeling.
   Tim has carols worth the stealing,
   Piping Tim of Galway.
   Thrush and linnet, finch and lark,
   To each other twitter "Hark!"
   Soon they sing from light to dark
   Pipings learnt in Galway.

HARRIGAN

Words and Music by George M. Cohan

THE GIRL I LEFT BEHIND ME

Traditional

1. The dames of France are fond and free, And Flemish lips are will - ing, And soft the maids of I - ta - ly, And Span - ish eyes are thrill - ing; Still though I bask be - neath their smile, Their charms fail to bind me, And my heart falls back to E - rin's Isle, To the girl I left be - hind me.

2. For she's as fair as Shan - non's side, And pur - er than its wat - er, But she re - fus'd to be my bride Though many a year I sough ther; Yet since to France I sail'd a - way, Her let - ters oft re - mind me, That I prom - is'd nev - er to gain - say The girl I left be - hind me.

3. She says "My own dear love, come home, My friends are rich and ma - ny, Or else a - broad with you I'll roam A sol - dier stout as an - y; If you'll not come, nor let me go, I'll think you have re - signed me;" My heart nigh broke when I an - swer'd "No" To the girl I left be - hind me.

4. For nev - er shall my true love brave A life of war and toil - ing, And nev - er as. a skulk - ing slave I'll tread my na - tive soil on; But were it free or to be freed, The bat - tle's close would find me, To Ire - land bound, nor mes - sage need From the girl I left be - hind me.

THE HAT MY FATHER WORE

Words and Music by Edwin Ferguson

CHORUS

It's old, but it's beau - ti - ful, The best was ev - er seen. 'Twas worn for more than nine - ty years, In that lit - tle Isle so green, From my fa - ther's great an - cest - ors it de - scen - ded, times ga - lore. It's a rel - ic of old Da - cin - cy, Is THE HAT MY FA - THER

1. WORE. It's WORE.

2. I

3. But

WORE.

THE HAT MY FATHER WORE UPON ST. PATRICK'S DAY

Words by William Jerome
Music by Jean Schwartz

CHORUS

I HAD FIFTEEN DOLLARS IN MY INSIDE POCKET

Words and Music by Harry Kennedy

I'LL TAKE YOU HOME AGAIN, KATHLEEN

Words and Music by Thomas P. Westendorf

Andante Moderato

1. I'll take you home a- gain, Kath -leen, a - cross the o - cean wild and wide, To
know you love me, Kath-leen, dear, your heart was ev- er fond and true; I
that dear home be- yond the sea, My Kath- leen shall a-gain re - turn, And

where your heart has ev - er been, Since first you were my bon - ny bride. The
al - ways feel when you are near That life holds noth- ing dear but you. The
when thy old friends wel-come thee, Thy lov - ing heart will cease to yearn. Where

I LOVE MY LOVE IN THE MORNING

By Gerald Griffin

* Play last four measures for Introduction or Interlude if desired

THE IRISHMAN'S SHANTY

Words and Music by Emmet Driscoll

THE IRISH EMIGRANT

Words by Lady Dufferin
Music by G. Barker

2. I'm very lonely now Mary, for the poor make no new friends,
But oh, they love the better still the few our Father sends.
And you were all I had, Mary, my blessing, and my pride,
There's nothing left to care for now, since my poor Mary died.
I'm bidding you a long farewell, my Mary kind and true,
But I'll not forget you, darlin', in the land I'm going to.
They say there's bread and work for all,
And the sun shines always there, but I'll ne'er forget old Ireland,
Were it fifty times as fair, were it fifty times as fair.

THE IRISH JUBILEE

Words by James Thornton
Music by Chas. Lawler

1. Oh, a short time a-go boys, an I-rish-man named Do-her-ty, Was e-
2. Cassi-dy at once sent out the in-vi-ta-tions, And
3. Blue-fish, Green-fish, Fish-hooks and par-tridg-es,
4. For des-sert we had tooth-picks, Ice-picks and skip-ping rope, And

lect-ed to the se-nate by a ve-ry large ma-jo-ri-ty, He felt so e-la-ted that he
ev'ry one that came was a cred-it to their na-tions, Some came on bi-cy-cles be-
Fish-balls, Snow-balls, Can-non-balls and Car-tridges, Then we ate Oat-meal till
washed them all down with a big piece of shav-ing soap, We ate ev-'ry thing that was

went to Den-nis Cas-si-dy, Who o-wned a bar-room of a ve-ry large ca-pac-i-ty,
cause they had no fare to pay, And those who did-n't come at all made up their minds to stay a-way,
we could hard-ly stir a-bout, Ketch-up and Hur-ry up, Sweet-krout and Sour-krout,
down on the bill of fare, Then looked on the back of it to see if a-ny more was there, Then the

twen-ty different languages, And don't for-get to tell them to bring their own sandwich-es; They've
ev-'ry chair was tak - en 'Till the front rooms and mushrooms were packed to suf-fo - ca - tion; When
Dear me and an-te-lope, And the wo - men eat so mushmellon, the men said they cant-a - lope;
be heard for miled a-round, When Gal - la-gher was in the air, his feet was nev-er on the ground; A

made me their sen - a - tor, and so to show my grat-i - tude, They'll have the fin - est sup-per ev - er
ev-'ry one was seat - ed, they start-ed to lay out the feast, Cas- si - dy said rise up and
Red Herrings, Smoked Herrings, Herrings from Old E-rin's Isle, Bo - log - na and fruit - cake, and
finer lot of danc - ers you nev - er set your eyes up on, And those who couldn't dance at all, were

giv-en in this lat - i - tude, Tell them the mu-sic will be furnished by O'- Raf-fer - ty, As-
give us each a cake of yeast, He then said, as man-a -ger he would try and fill the chair, We
sau-sa - ges a half a mile, There was hot corn and cold corn, corn salve and Hon-ey comb,
danc-ing with their slip-pers on, Some danced Jig-step, Door steps and highland flings, And

ISLE O' DREAMS

Words by Geo. Graff, Jr. and Chauncey Olcott
Music by Ernest R. Ball

KITTY OF COLERAINE

By Edward Lysaght

I'VE GOT RINGS ON MY FINGERS

Words by Weston and Barnes
Music by Maurice Scott

JOLLY IRISHMEN

Words and Music by William Carleton

Mike and Dan, and Ma-ry Ann and Pat Mc Cann, There was Toole, the
fought and dhrunk, and dhrank and fought, and fought and dhrank, They dhrank and
wine and punch, and I-rish spuds all in their duds, There was knives and

fool, and Pat Drum-goole and me. We
fought, bowld I-rish-men wur they. They had a row that ver-y night, And
forks, and gin-ger-beer and tay. But they

put the wo-men in a fright. There was mur-dher right and tight, And all the boys be-gan to fight.

CHORUS

Hur roo! boys, here we are a-gin! Here we are a-gin! here we are a-gin! Hur-roo! boys,

here we are a-gin, Bowld I-rish-men are we. Hur- we. 2. Pat we.
3. The

KATHLEEN MAVOURNEEN

Words by Annie Crawford
Music by Frederick W. Nicolls Crouch

★ The original music to the 2nd Verse is different in places

THE KERRY DANCE

Words and Music by J. L. Molloy

Brightly

Oh, the days of the Ker - ry danc - ing! Oh, the ring of the pi - per's tune! Oh, for one of those hours of glad - ness, gone, a - las! like our youth, too soon! When the boys be - gan to gath - er in the glen of a sum - mer night,

THE LAST ROSE OF SUMMER

By Thomas Moore

Slowly with expression

*Play the first four measures with up beat for introduction.

LET ERIN REMEMBER THE DAYS OF OLD

Words by Thomas Moore
Music From The Air "The Red Fox"

1. Let Erin remember the days of old, Ere her faithless sons betray'd her; When
2. On Lough Neagh's bank, as the fisherman strays, When the clear cold eve's declining, He

1. Malachi wore the collar of gold, Which he won from the proud invader; When her
2. sees the round tow'rs of other days In the wave beneath him shining; Thus shall

1. kings, with standard of green unfurl'd, Led the Red Branch knights to danger; Ere the
2. mem'ry often, in dreams sublime, Catch a glimpse of the days that are over; Thus

1. em'rald gem of the western world Was set in the crown of a stranger.
2. sighing, look thro' the waves of Time For the long faded glories they cover.

LET ME CALL YOU SWEETHEART

Words by Beth Slater Whitson
Music by Leo Friedman

LITTLE ANNIE ROONEY

Words and Music by Michael Nolan

A win - ning way, a pleas - ant smile, Dress'd so neat but
The par - lor's small but neat and clean, And set with taste so
We've been en - gaged close on a year, The hap - py time is

quite in style, Mer - ry chaff your time to while, Has
sel - dom seen, And you can bet the house - hold queen Is
draw - ing near, I'll wed the one I love so dear,

lit - tle An - nie Roon - ey; Ev - 'ry ev' - ning, rain or
lit - tle An - nie Roon - ey! The fire burns cheer - ful - ly and
lit - tle An - nie Roon - ey! My friends de - clare I am in

LONDONDERRY AIR

Traditional

Andante *(con espressione)*

Would God I were the ten-der ap-ple blos-som ____ That floats and
Yea, would to God I were a-mong the ros - es ____ That lean to

falls from off the twist-ed bough, ___ To lie and faint with-in your silk-en
kiss you as you float be - tween, ___ While on the low - est branch a bud un-

bo - som, with-in your silk-en bo - som, As that does now! ____ Or would I
clos - es, a bud ___ un - clos - es, To touch you, queen. ____ Nay, since you

poco rit.   *a tempo*

were a lit-tle bur-nish'd ap-ple ___ For you to pluck me, glid-ing by so
will not love, would I were grow-ing, ___ A hap-py dai - sy, in the gar-den

cold, ___ While sun and shade your robe of lawn will dap - ple, ___ your robe of
path; ___ That so your sil - ver foot might press me go - ing, ___ might press me

lawn, And your hair's spun gold. ___
go - ing ev - en un - to

death. ___

MARY'S A GRAND OLD NAME

Words and Music by George M. Cohan

Mc SORLEY'S TWINS

Words and Music by Gustave Phillips

4th Verse: Thin, Mrs. Mc Sorley jumped up in a rage,
And she threatened Miss Mullinses' life;
Says ould Denny Mullins, "I'll bate the firsht man
That'd dare lay a hand on me wife!"
The Mc Ganns and the Geoghans, they had an ould grudge,
And Mag Murphy pitched into the Flynns;
They fought like the divil, turned over the bed,
And they smothered the poor little twins. *Chorus:*

THE MINSTREL BOY

Words by Thomas Moore
Music From the Air "The Moreen"

2. Minstrel fell! But the foeman's chain
   Could not bring that proud soul under;
   The harp he lov'd ne'er spoke again,
   For he tore its chords asunder;
   And said "No chains shall sully thee,
   Thou soul of love and bravery!
   Thy songs were made for the pure and free,
   They shall never sound in slavery."

MOLLY MALONE (Cockles and Mussels)

Words and Music by Martin Corrigan

MOLLY O!

Words and Music by Wm. J. Scanlan

Valse tempo

1. She's plain Mol-ly O, _____ sim-ple and sweet, _____
2. Brave sol-diers may war, _____ he-roes may die, _____

My heart is gone, _____ I lay me at her feet; _____
With Mol-ly, dear, _____ the world I would de-fy; _____

So light her tread, _____ so fond her gaze, _____
Ten-der her heart, _____ lov-ing and true, _____

Who would not love my Mol-ly dear? _____
Flow'rs of the val-ley call her queen! _____

MOTHER MACHREE

Words by Rida Johnson Young
Music by Chauncey Olcott and Ernest R. Ball

Allegretto, ma espressivo

There's a spot in my heart which no col-leen may own, There's a
Ev-'ry sor-row or care in the dear days gone by, Was made

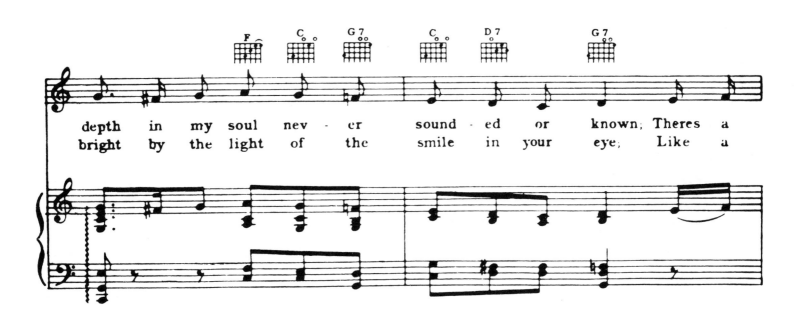

depth in my soul nev-er sound-ed or known; There's a
bright by the light of the smile in your eye; Like a

MY MELANCHOLY BABY

Words by George A. Norton
Music by Ernie Burnett

MY BEAUTIFUL IRISH MAID

Words and Music by Chauncey Olcott

1. We stand to-geth-er, you and I, Where we stood years a-go,_____ Be-neath the same blue I-rish sky, Our
2. I know the love you gave me then Is just as fond and true,_____ Those eyes of yours speak hope a-gain, Sweet

hearts with joy a - glow._____ You prom - ised, then, you
eyes of I - rish blue!_____ I know you'll keep your

would be mine, In all your charms ar - rayed;_____ I'm here to
prom - ise, love, Tho' stars a - bove may fade!_____ Thro' storm and

claim you for my own, My pret - ty I - rish maid!_____
shine I've come to you, My pret - ty I - rish maid!_____

CHORUS

Oh! my love,_____ how I've wait-ed and long'd_ for

MY WILD IRISH ROSE

Words and Music by Chauncey Olcott

If you lis - ten, I'll sing you a sweet lit - tle song Of a flow - er that's now drooped and dead. _____ Yet _ dear - er to me, Yes, than all of its mates, Though each holds a - loft its proud head. _____ 'Twas giv - en to me by a girl that I know, Since we've met, faith, I've known no re - pose. _____ She is

dear - er by far Than the world's bright - est star, And I call her my wild I - rish

OFF TO PHILADELPHIA

Traditional

1. My name is Pad-dy Lea-ry, From a *shpot* call'd Tip-per-a-ry, The
2. There's a girl call'd Kate Ma-lone,__ Whom I'd hop'd to call my own,__ And to
3. When they told me I must leave the place, I tried to keep a cheer-ful face, For to

1. hearts of all the girls I am a thorn__ in, But be-
2. see my lit-tle cab-in floor a-dorn__-in', But my
3. show my heart's deep sor-row I was scorn__-in', But the

1. fore the break of morn,__ *Faith!* 'tis they'll be all for-lorn,__ For Im
2. heart is sad and wea-ry, How can she be Mis-sis Lea-ry, If I
3. tears will sure-ly blind me For the friends I *lave* be-hind me, When I

CHORUS

O KATY O'NEIL

Words and Music by Edward Rupert

O Ka-ty O'-Neil, how can I con-ceal the way that I feel in my heart? The wa-ters that flow and the breez-es that blow all bid me to go where thou art.

CHORUS

2. I feel a sweet pain again and again.
Say not 'tis in vain that I pray,
The time will soon be when you will agree
Forever with me love to stay.

Chorus: Sure I always ponder as lonely I wander
How sad 'tis that we are apart.
O Katy O'Neil, how can I conceal
The way that I feel in my heart?

3. Far over the sea be waiting for me,
And soon shall I come there to you.
So Katy don't marry but stay there and tarry
Until time shall carry me through.

Chorus: Sure I always ponder as lonely I wander
How foolish it is we're apart.
O Katy O'Neil, how can I conceal
The way that I feel in my heart?

OLCOTT'S LULLABY

Words and Music by Chauncey Olcott

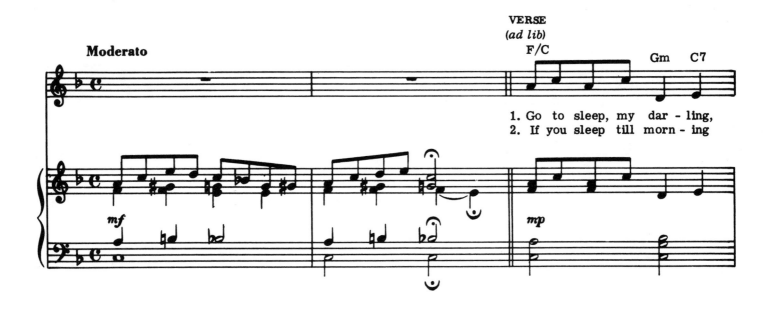

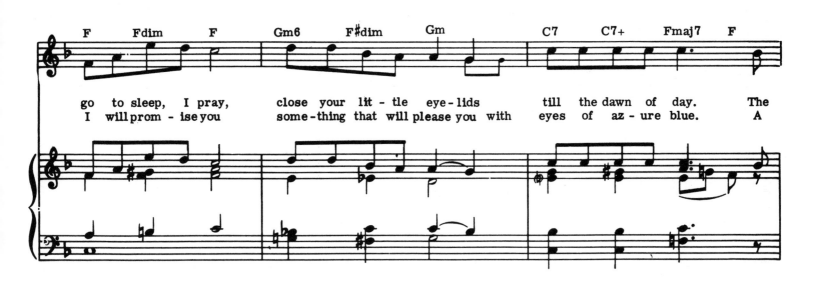

near._____ An - gels flit_____ a - bout

you, thru your sweet lit - tle dreams,_____

while the light___ from heav - en sheds its ra -

diant beams._____ Then beams._____

NORAH, THE PRIDE OF KILDARE

Words and Music by John Parry

* Play the last four measures for Introduction or Interlude if desired

PAT MALLOY

Words and Music by Dion Boucicault

A PLACE IN THY MEMORY

Words and Music by Gerald Griffin

oth - er may woo_____ thee near - er, an - oth - er may____ win_____ and____ wear; I____ care not though____ he____ be____ dear - er if____ thou____ but re - mem - ber me there.

2. Remember me not as a lover
Whose hope, whose hope was cross'd;
Whose bosom can never recover
The light it hath lost:
As the young bride remembers
The mother she loves,
Tho' she never may see;
As a sister remembers a brother,
Oh! dearest, remember me.

3. Could I be thy true lover, dearest,
Could'st thou, could'st thou smile on me,
I would be the fondest and nearest
That ever lov'd thee!
But a cloud on my pathway is glooming,
That never must burst upon thine;
And heaven that made thee all blooming,
Ne'er made thee to wither on mine.

4. Remember me then, Oh! remember
My calm, my calm, light love,
Though bleak as the blasts of November,
My life may prove, that life will,
Though lonely be sweet,
If its brightest enjoyment should be,
A smile and kind word when we meet,
And a place in thy memory.

RORY O'MOORE

Words and Music by Samuel Lover

1. Young Ror-y O' Moore court-ed Kath-leen Bawn, he was bold as a hawk, she as soft as the dawn, he___

wish'd in his heart pret-ty Kath-leen to please, and he thought the best way to do that was to tease. "Now

Ror-y be ais-y," sweet Kath-leen would cry, re-proof on her lips, but a smile in her eye, "with your

tricks I don't know, in troth, what I'm a-bout, Faith, you've teas'd till I've put on my coat in-side out." "Och,—

jew-el," says Ror-y, "that same is the way you've treat-ed my heart for this man-y a day, and 'tis

pleas'd that I am, and why not, to be sure? For 'tis all for good luck," says bold Ror-y O' Moore.

2. "Indeed then, "says Kathleen," don't think of the like,
For I have gave a promise to soothering Mike;
The ground that I walk on, he loves, I'll be bound, "
"Faith, " says Rory, "I'd rather love you than the ground. "
"Now Rory, I'll cry if you don't let me go,
Sure I dhrame every night that I'm hating you so;"
"Och, " says Rory, "that same I'm delighted to hear,
For dhrames always go by conthraries, my dear;
So, jewel, keep dhramin' that same till you die,
Bright mornin' will give dirty night the black lie,
And 'tis pleas'd that I am, and why not, to be sure,
Since 'tis all for good luck," sings bold Rory O'Moore.

3. "Arrah, Kathleen, my darlint, you've teas'd me enough,
Since I've thrash'd for your sake Dinny Grimes and Jim Duff,
And I've made myself, dhrinking your health, quite a baste,
So I think after that I may talk to the priest."
Then Rory, the rogue, stole his arm round her neck,
So soft and so white, without freckle or speck,
And he look'd in her eyes that were beaming with light,
And he kiss'd her sweet lips, don't you think he was right?
Now Rory, leave off, sir, you'll hug me no more,
That's eight times today that you've kiss'd me before!"
"Then here goes another, " says he, "to make sure,
For there's luck in odd numbers, " says Rory O'Moore.

THE ROSE OF TRALEE

Words by C. Mordaunt Spender
Music by Charles W. Glover

ST. PATRICK'S DAY

Words and Music by M. J. Barry

Allegro

1. Oh! blest be the days when the Green Ban-ner float-ed, sub-lime o'er the moun-tains of free In-nis-fail, when her sons, to her glo-ry and free-dom de-vot-ed, de-fied the in-vad-er to tread her soil; when back o'er the main they chased the Dane, and gave to re-li-gion and learn-ing their spoil, when

2. Her sceptre, alas! passed away to the stranger,
And treason surrendered what valor had held;
But true hearts remained amid darkness and danger,
Which, spite of her tyrants, would not be quelled.
Oft, oft through the night flashed gleams of light,
Which almost the darkness of bondage dispelled,
But a star now is near, her heaven to cheer,
Not like the wild gleams which so fitfully darted,
But long to shine down with its hallowing ray,
On daughters as fair, and sons as truehearted,
As Erin beholds on Saint Patrick's Day.

3. Oh! blest be the hour when, begirt by her cannon,
And hailed as it rose by a nation's applause,
That flag waved aloft o'er the spire of Dungannon,
Asserting, for Irishmen, Irish laws.
Once more shall it wave o'er hearts as brave,
Despite of the dastards who mock at her cause,
And like brothers agreed, whatever their creed,
Her children, inspired by those glories departed,
No longer in darkness desponding will stay,
But join in the cause like the brave and truehearted,
Who rise for their rights on Saint Patrick's Day

SWEET ROSIE O'GRADY

Words and Music by Maud Nugent

Andante moderato

Just down a-round the cor-ner of the street where I re-side, There
I nev-er shall for-get the day she prom-ised to be mine, As

lives the cut-est lit-tle girl that I have ev-er spied; Her
we sat tell-ing love-tales, in the gold-en sum-mer time. 'Twas

name is Rose O' Gra-dy and, I don't mind tell-ing you,
on her fing-er that I placed a small en-gage-ment ring,

she's the sweet-est lit-tle Rose the gar-den ev-er grew.
in the trees, the lit-tle birds this song they seemed to sing:

Chorus: Valse moderato

Sweet Ro-sie O' Gra - - dy, My dear lit-tle

Rose,_____ She's my stead-y la - dy,

ST. PATRICK WAS A GENTLEMAN

By Henry Bennet and Mr. Toleken

★ Play the first eight measures for Introduction or Interlude if desired

THEY SAIL'D AWAY (Dublin Bay)

Words by Annie Crawford
Music by George Baker

* Play the last four measures for Introduction or Interlude if desired

THO' THE LAST GLIMPSE OF ERIN (The Coulin)

Traditional

Andante con espressione

1. Tho' the last glimpse of E - rin with
2. To the gloom of some des - ert or
3. And I'll gaze on thy gold hair, as

1. sor - row I see, Yet wher - ev - er thou art shall seem
2. cold rock - y shore, Where the eye of the stran - ger can
3. grace - ful it wreathes, And hang o'er thy soft harp as

1. E - rin to me; In ex - ile thy bo - som shall still be my
2. haunt us no more, I will fly with my Cou - lin, and think the rough
3. wild - ly it breathes; Nor dread that the cold - heart - ed Sax - on will

poco cresc.

1. home, And thine eyes make my cli - mate wher - ev - er we roam.
2. wind Less rude than the foes we leave frown - ing be - hind.
3. tear One chord from that harp, or one lock from that hair.

dim. *p* *poco rit.* D.C.

WEARING OF THE GREEN

Words by Dion Boucicault
Music From the Scotch Air "The Tulip" by Oswald

1. Oh Pad-dy, dear, and did you hear the news that's go-in' round? The
Sham-rock is for-bid by law to grow on I-rish ground. Saint
Pat-rick's day no more to keep, his col-or can't be seen, for

113

2. Then since the colour we must wear is England's cruel red,
   Sure Ireland's son's will ne'er forget the blood that they have shed;
   You may pull the Shamrock from your hat, and cast it on the sod,
   But 'twill take root and flourish there, tho' underfoot 'tis trod!
   When laws can stop the blades of grass from growin' as they grow,
   And when the leaves in summertime their verdure dare not show,
   Then I will change the colour too, I wear in my caubeen,
   But till that day, plaze God! I'll stick-to wearin' o' the green!   Chorus:

3. But if at last our colour should be torn from Ireland's heart,
   Her sons, with shame and sorrow, from the dear ould Isle will part;
   I've heard a whisper of a land that lies beyond the sea,
   Where rich and poor stand equal in the light of Freedom's day.
   Ah, Erin! must we leave you, driven by a tyrant's hand.
   Must we seek a mother's blessing from a strange and distant land?
   Where the cruel cross of England shall never more be seen,
   And where, plaze God we'll live and die, still wearin' o' the green!   Chorus:

WHEN IT'S MOONLIGHT IN MAYO
(Two Irish Eyes Are Shining)

Words by Jack Mahoney
Music by Percy Wenrich

It's just a year a-go to-day I left old Er-in's Isle, My

Her I-rish eyes like bea-cons shine on thro' the dark-est night, I

heart was throb-bing in the sun-light of my col-leen's smile; In
know their sweet love-beams will al-ways fill the world with light; The

all my dreams I hear her sweet voice call-ing soft and low, I
ros-es on her cheeks will lend en-chant-ment to the scene, And

know she's wait-ing where we said "good-bye" in old Ma-yo.
when the sham-rocks wed the dew, I'll wed my sweet col-leen.

CHORUS Moderato

Now two I-rish eyes are shin-ing,_____ And an

WE MAY ROAM THRO' THIS WORLD
(The Daughters Of Erin)

Words by Thomas Moore
Music From The Air "Garryowen"

1. We may roam thro' this world, like a child at a feast, Who but sips of a sweet, and then flies to the rest, And when pleas-ure be-gins to grow dull in the east, We may or-der our wings and be off to the west; But if hearts that feel and

2. In England the gar-den of beau-ty is kept By a drag-on of prud-er-y plac'd with-in call; But so oft this un-a-mia-ble drag-on has slept, That the gar-den's but care-less-ly watched aft-er all. Oh! they want the wild sweet

3. In France, when the heart of a wom-an sets sail, On the o-cean of wed-lock its for-tune to try; Love sel-dom goes far in a ves-sel so frail, But pi-lot's her off, and then bids her good-bye. While the daugh-ters of E-rin

WHEN FIRST I SAW SWEET PEGGY (The Low Back'd Car)

Words and Music by Samuel Lover

Allegro

1. When first I saw sweet Peg - gy, 'twas on a mar - ket day; a
2. In bat - tles wide com - mo - tion, the proud and might - y Mars; with

low back'd car she drove and sat up - on a truss of hay; but
hos - tile scythes de - mands his tythes of death in war - like cars: but

when that hay was bloom - ing grass and deck'd with flow'rs of spring. No
Peg - gy peace - ful god - dess, has darts in her bright eye, that

3. Sweet Peggy round her car, sir!
   Has strings of ducks and geese,
   But scores of hearts she slaughters,
   By far out number these:
   While she among her poultry sits,
   Just like a turtle dove,
   Well worth the cage, I do engage,
   Of the blooming god of love!
   While she sits in her low back'd car,
   The lovers come near and far,
   And envy the chicken, that Peggy is pickin'
   While she sits in her low back'd car.

4. I'd rather own that car, sir!
   With Peggy by my side,
   Than a coach and four, and gold galore
   And a lady for my bride:
   For the lady would sit forminst me,
   On a cushion made with taste,
   While Peggy would be beside me,
   With my arm around her waist
   As we drove in her low back'd car,
   To be married by Father Maher,
   Oh, my heart would beat high,
   At her glance and her sigh,
   Tho' it beat in a low back'd car!

WHEN I DREAM OF OLD ERIN (I'm Dreaming Of You)

Words by Marvin Lee
Music by Leo Friedman

Chorus Andantino moderato

When I dream of old E - rin I'm dream - ing of you, With your

sweet, rogu - ish smile and your true eyes of blue, For my

love, like the Sham - rock, each day strong - er grew; When I

dream of old E - rin, I'm dream - ing of you.

WHERE DID YOU GET THAT HAT?

Words and Music by Jos. J. Sullivan

1. Now how I came to get this hat 'tis ver-y strange and fun-ny: Grand-fa-ther died and left to me his
2. If I go to the op-'ra-house, in the op-'ra sea-son, there's some-one___ sure to shout at me, with-
3. At twen-ty one I thought I would to my sweet-heart be mar-ried; The peo-ple___ in the neigh-bor-hood had

Is - n't it a nob - by one, and just the prop - er style?

I should like to have one just the same as that! Wher-

e'er I go they shout: *"Hel - lo! Where did you get that hat?"

*Shout

WHERE THE RIVER SHANNON FLOWS

Words and Music by James L. Russell

mo - ment that I meet her with a hug and kiss I'll greet her, For there's

not a col - leen sweet - er, Where the Riv - er Shan - non flows.

Sure no flows.

WHO THREW THE OVERALLS IN MISTRESS MURPHY'S CHOWDER?

Words and Music by George L. Giefer

VERSE

1. Mis - tress Mur - phy gave a par - ty, just a - bout a week a -
2. (They___) dragged the pants from out the soup, and laid them on the

go, Ev - 'ry - thing was plen - ti - ful, the Mur-phys they're not slow. They
floor, Each man swore up - on his life, he'd ne'er seen them be - fore, They were

treat - ed us like gen - tle - men, we tried to act the same, On - ly for what
plas - tered up with mor - tar, and were worn out at the knee, They had their man - y

MY ISLE OF GOLDEN DREAMS

Words by Gus Kahn
Music by Walter Blaufuss

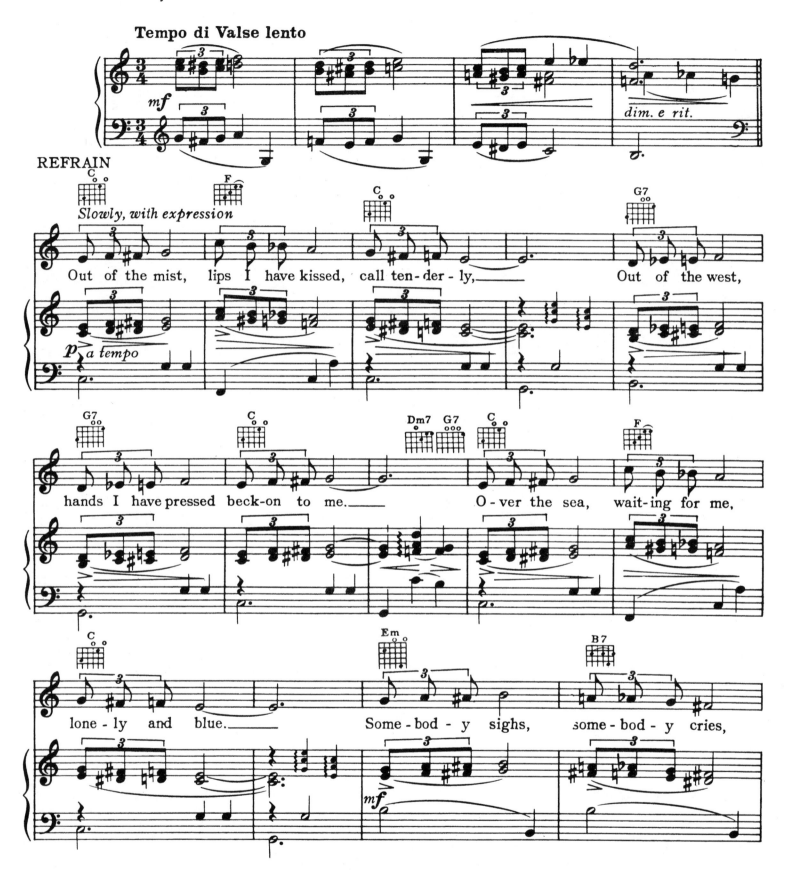

TOO-RA-LOO-RA-LOO-RAL
(That's An Irish Lullaby)

Words and Music by J. R. Shannon

simple lit - tle dit - ty, In her good ould I - rish way, And I'd
hear her voice a hum - min' To me as in days of yore, When she

give the world if she could sing That song to me this day.
used to rock me fast a - sleep Out - side the cab - in door.

REFRAIN *Smoothly with much expression*

Too - ra - loo - ra - loo - ral, Too - ra - loo - ra - li,

mp in time

WIDOW MACHREE

Words and Music by Samuel Lover

Verse 1:
Wid-ow Ma-chree, 'tis no won-der you frown, *Och hone!* Wid-ow Ma-chree, *Faith* it ru-ins your looks, that same dir-ty black gown, *Och hone!* Wid-ow Ma-chree! How al-ter'd your air, With that close cap you wear, 'Tis de-stroy-ing your hair That should be flow-ing free, Be no lon-ger a churl Of its black silk-en curl, *Och hone!* Wid-ow Ma-chree!

Verse 2:
Wid-ow Ma-chree now the sum-mer is come, *Och hone!* Wid-ow Ma-chree, When ev-'ry-thing smiles should a beau-ty look glum? *Och hone!* Wid-ow Ma-chree, See the birds go in pairs, And the rab-bits and hares, Why e-ven the bears Now in coup-les a-gree, And the mute lit-tle fish Tho' they can't *spake*, they wish, *Och hone!* Wid-ow Ma-chree!

Verse 3:
Wid-ow Ma-chree, and when win-ter comes in, *Och hone!* Wid-ow Ma-chree, To be pok-ing the fire all a-lone is a sin, *Och hone!* Wid-ow Ma-chree, Why the shov-el and tongs, To each oth-er be-longs, And the kit-tle sings songs Full of fam-i-ly glee; While a-lone with your cup, Like a her-mit you sup, *Och hone!* Wid-ow Ma-chree!

Verse 4:
How do you know, with the com-forts I've *towld*, *Och hone!* Wid-ow Ma-chree, But you're keep-ing some poor fel-low out in the *cowld*, *Och hone!* Wid-ow Ma-chree, With such sins on your head, Sure you're peace would be fled, Could you sleep in your bed With-out think-ing to see Some ghost or some sprite, That would wake you each night, Cry-ing, *Och hone!* Wid-ow Ma-chree!

Verse 5:
Take my ad-vice, dar-ling Wid-ow Ma-chree, *Och hone!* Wid-ow Ma-chree, And with my ad-vice, *faith* I wish you'd take me, *Och hone!* Wid-ow Ma-chree, You'd have me to de-sire Then to stir up the fire, And sure hope is no li-ar In whis-p'ring to me That the ghosts would de-part When you'd me near your heart, *Och hone!* Wid-ow Ma-chree!

* Play the last four measures for Introduction or Interlude if desired

WHEN IRISH EYES ARE SMILING

Words by Chauncey Olcott and Geo. Graff, Jr.
Music by Ernest R. Ball

143

IF I KNOCK THE "L" KELLY
(It Would Still Be Kelly To Me)

Words by Sam M. Lewis and Joe Young
Music by Bert Grant

mis-spelled the name; In-stead of Kel-ly with doub-le "L - Y,"
Kel-ly you are; Shame on you Clan-cy, just see what you've done,

He paint-ed Kel-ly, but one "L" was shy, Pat said, "it looks right, but
You've spoiled the name of an Ir-ish-man's son;" "Don't let an "L" come bet-

I want no pay, I've reas-oned it out in my own lit-tle way."
-ween us," said Pat, "I've fig-ur-ed it out like a real dip-lo-mat."

If I knock the "L" out of Kel-ly, ___ It would still be

sfz p-f   sfz

Kel-ly to me; ____ Sure a sin-gle "L - Y" or a doub-le "L - Y," Should

look just the same to an Ir-ish-man's eye. Knock off an "L" from Kil-lar-ney,

____ Still Kil - lar-ney it al-ways will be, But if I knock the "L" out of

Kel -ly, ____ Sure he'd knock the "L" out of me. If I me.

M-O-T-H-E-R
(A Word That Means The World To Me)

Lyric by Howard Johnson
Music by Theodore Morse

fail, if they were called up-on a sim-ple word to spell. Now if you'd like to put me to a
folks were ver - y proud of me, for "Moth-er" was the word. Al-though I'll nev - er lay a claim to

test,_____ There's one dear name that I can spell the best:_____
fame,_____ I'm sat - is -fied that I can spell the name:_____

CHORUS

"M" is for the mil - lion things she gave me,
is for the mer - cy she pos - ses - ses,

"O" means on - ly that she's grow - ing old,_____
means that I owe her all I own,_____

150

ROSES OF PICARDY

Words by Fred E. Weatherly
Music by Hayden Wood

Brightly

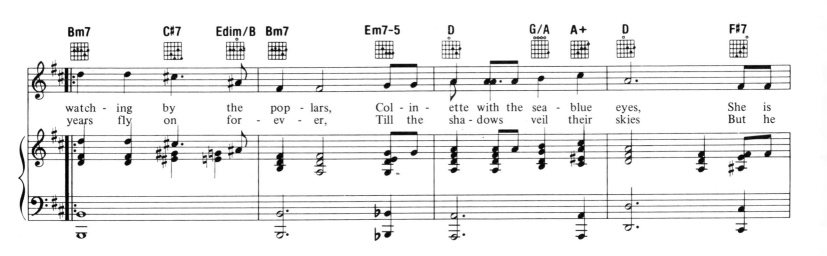

MACNAMARA'S BAND

Words by John J. Stamford
Music by Shamus O'Connor

IRELAND MUST BE HEAVEN
(For My Mother Came From There)

Words and Music by Joseph McCarthy, Howard Johnson and Fred Fisher

160

BE SURE AND KISS THE BLARNEY STONE

Words by George Graff, Jr.
Music by George H. Gartlan

163

ALICE BLUE GOWN

Lyric by Joseph McCarthy
Music by Harry Tierney

(The) BELLS OF ST. MARY'S

Words by Douglas Furber
Music by A. Emmett Adams

IF YOU WERE THE ONLY GIRL IN THE WORLD

Words by Clifford Grey
Music by Nat D. Ayer

I'M ALWAYS CHASING RAINBOWS

Lyric by Joseph McCarthy
Music by Harry Carroll

IRENE

Lyric by Joseph McCarthy
Music by Harry Tierney

K-K-K-KATY

Words and Music by Geoffrey O'Hara

IT TAKES A GREAT BIG IRISH HEART TO SING AN IRISH SONG

Words by Al Herman
Music by Jack Glogau

Ev - 'ry - where I go, I'm sure to hear That
Sure, you've heard that sweet old mel - o - dy,

sweet mel - o - dy,____ "Moth - er Ma - chree,"____
songs we all know____ From Coun - ty Ma - yo,____

CHORUS Allegro Moderato

Sure, it takes a great big I-rish heart To

sing an I-rish song, _____ An I-rish tune with

all those en-dear-ing charms, And a voice that's sweet and

strong; _____ Jip, Jip, my lit-tle horse, sure, that's a
Sung, by an I-rish-man, sure, that's worth

185

LET THE REST OF THE WORLD GO BY

Words by J. Keirn Brennan
Music by Ernest R. Ball

THERE'S SOMETHING IN THE NAME OF IRELAND
(That The Whole World Seems To Love)

Lyric by Howard Johnson
Music by Milton Ager

THEY GO WILD, SIMPLY WILD, OVER ME

Lyric by Joseph McCarthy
Music by Fred Fisher

Brightly

Verse

1. I hate to talk a-bout my-self, but here's one time I must; Your
2. (I) get so man-y pret-ty girls, I give a few a-way; They

con - fi - dence I'll trust, I have to speak or bust. It's
both - er me each day, There're lead - ing me a - stray. There's

fun - ny how I get the girls, I nev - er try at all; I
lots of fel - lows go with girls and nev - er get their drift; I